REALLY EASY JAZZIN' ABOUT

PIANO/KEYBOARD

PAM WEDGWOOD

† There are three CD tracks for each piece: a complete performance,
a backing track, and the backing track at a slower tempo.
A count-in of two bars is given before all the tracks.

FaberＭ**ff** MUSIC

2

Track 1

You can use a funky drum beat with this one.

Pam Wedgwood

PING-PONG

You can try a dixieland beat to this piece.

for Clementine

In the eyes of a tiger

You can try a disco drum beat with this piece.

Dual Control

You can use a medium rock beat with this piece.

6

Hot Chilli

You can use a samba rhythm with this piece.

Hip-hop

You can use an 8-beat pop rhythm with this piece.

Lively, with fun ♩ = 132

Garage Sale

You can use a heavy rock rhythm with this piece.

Wise Guy

You can use a jazz waltz rhythm with this piece.

Night Patrol

You can use a medium 8-beat rhythm with this piece.

Popcorn

You can use a relaxed swing rhythm with this piece.

Your First Hit Single

You can use a rock 'n' roll beat with this piece.

D. C. al ⊕ poi al Coda

CODA

Big Chief Little Foot

A chance for you to use the pedal on the right.

Moonlight Shadows

You can use a slow ballad accompaniment with this piece.

for Stuart

THE JUMPING BEAN

You can try a disco beat with this piece.

Jammy Dodger

You can use a ragtime rhythm with this piece.

WASHING-UP BLUES

You can use a slow swing beat with this piece.

The Swinging Sisters

You can use a swing beat with this piece.

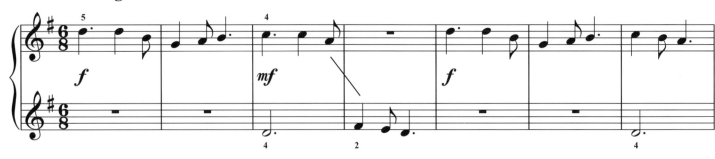

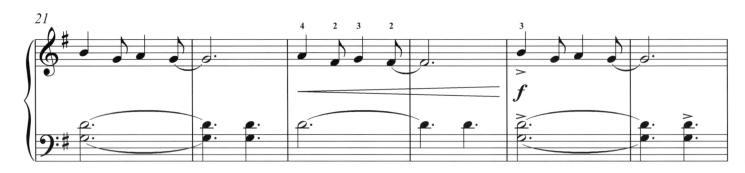

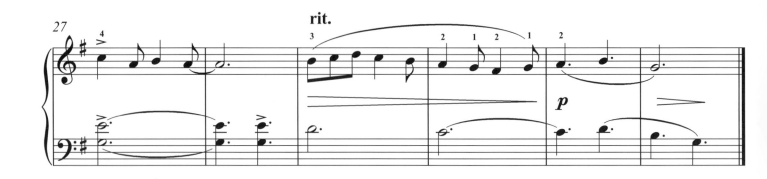

A sad little tale

You can use a slow waltz beat with this piece.

Spell it out to me, Baby!

You can use a swing rhythm with this piece.

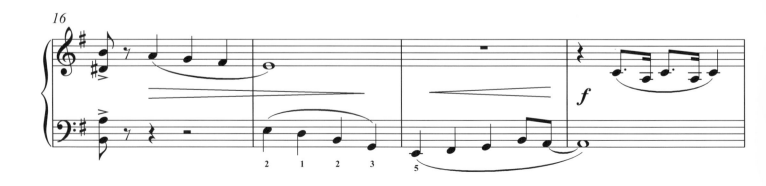

The JAZZIN' ABOUT series
PAM WEDGWOOD

Jazzin' About. Trumpet	ISBN 0-571-51039-6
Jazzin' About. Trombone	ISBN 0-571-56943-9
Jazzin' About. Alto Saxophone	ISBN 0-571-51054-X
Jazzin' About. Piano	ISBN 0-571-51105-8
Jazzin' About. Clarinet	ISBN 0-571-51273-9
Jazzin' About. Flute	ISBN 0-571-51275-5
Jazzin' About. Violin	ISBN 0-571-51315-8
Jazzin' About. Cello	ISBN 0-571-51316-6
Jazzin' About. Piano duet	ISBN 0-571-51662-9
Green Jazzin' About. Piano	ISBN 0-571-51645-9
Easy Jazzin' About. Piano	ISBN 0-571-51337-9
Easy Jazzin' About. Piano duet	ISBN 0-571-51661-0
Easy Jazzin' About. Descant Recorder	ISBN 0-571-52329-3
More Jazzin' About. Piano	ISBN 0-571-51437-5
Christmas Jazzin' About. Piano duet	ISBN 0-571-51584-3
Christmas Jazzin' About. Clarinet	ISBN 0-571-51585-1
Christmas Jazzin' About. Flute	ISBN 0-571-51586-X
Christmas Jazzin' About. Violin	ISBN 0-571-51694-7
Christmas Jazzin' About. Cello	ISBN 0-571-51695-5
Christmas Jazzin' About. Trumpet	ISBN 0-571-51696-3
Really Easy Jazzin' About. Piano	ISBN 0-571-52089-8
Really Easy Jazzin' About. Flute	ISBN 0-571-52097-9
Really Easy Jazzin' About. Clarinet	ISBN 0-571-52098-7
Really Easy Jazzin' About. Oboe	ISBN 0-571-52124-X
Really Easy Jazzin' About. Bassoon	ISBN 0-571-52138-X
Really Easy Jazzin' About. Trombone	ISBN 0-571-52139-8
Really Easy Jazzin' About. Horn	ISBN 0-571-52172-X
Really Easy Jazzin' About. Alto Saxophone	ISBN 0-571-52197-5
Really Easy Jazzin' About. Trumpet	ISBN 0-571-52198-3
Really Easy Jazzin' About. Violin	ISBN 0-571-52201-7
Really Easy Jazzin' About. Recorder	ISBN 0-571-52408-7
Really Easy Jazzin' About Studies. Piano	ISBN 0-571-52422-2
Jazzin' About. Piano (with CD)	ISBN 0-571-53400-7
More Jazzin' About. Piano (with CD)	ISBN 0-571-53401-5
Easy Jazzin' About. Piano (with CD)	ISBN 0-571-53402-3
Really Easy Jazzin' About. Piano (with CD)	ISBN 0-571-53403-1
Christmas Jazzin' About. Piano (with CD)	ISBN 0-571-53404-X
Jazzin' About Styles. Piano (with CD)	ISBN 0-571-53405-8
Jazzin' About Standards. Piano (with CD)	ISBN 0-571-53406-6
Easy Jazzin' About Standards. Piano (with CD)	ISBN 0-571-53407-4

© 2001 by Faber Music Ltd
First published in 2001 by Faber Music Ltd
Bloomsbury House 74–77 Great Russell Street London WC1B 3DA
Cover by Velladesign
Music engraved by MusicSet 2000
Printed in England by Caligraving Ltd
All rights reserved

ISBN10: 0-571-53403-1
EAN13: 978-0-571-53403-6

To buy Faber Music publications or to find out about the full range of titles available
please contact your local music retailer or Faber Music sales enquiries:

Faber Music Limited, Burnt Mill, Elizabeth Way, Harlow, CM20 2HX England
Tel: +44 (0)1279 82 89 82   Fax: +44 (0)1279 82 89 83
sales@fabermusic.com   fabermusic.com